BUG BOOKS

Centipede

Karen Hartley, Chris Macro and Philip Taylor

www.heinemann.co.uk/library
Visit our website to find out more information about Heinemann Library books.

To order:
 Phone 44 (0) 1865 888066
 Send a fax to 44 (0) 1865 314091
 Visit the Heinemann Bookshop at www.heinemann.co.uk/library to browse our catalogue and order online.

First published in Great Britain by Heinemann Library, Halley Court, Jordan Hill, Oxford OX2 8EJ, part of Harcourt Education.
Heinemann is a registered trademark of Harcourt Education Ltd.

Editorial: Clare Lewis and Katie Shepherd
Design: Ron Kamen, Michelle Lisseter and Bridge Creative Services Limited
Illustrations: Alan Fraser at Pennant Illustration
Picture Research: Maria Joannou
Production: Helen McCreath

Printed and bound in China by South China Printers

10 digit ISBN 0 431 01839 1
13 digit ISBN 978 0 431 01839 3
10 09 08 07 06
10 9 8 7 6 5 4 3 2 1

British Library Cataloguing in Publication Data
Hartley, Karen
Bug Books: Centipede - 2nd Edition
595.6'2
A full catalogue record for this book is available from the British Library.

Acknowledgements
The publishers would like to thank the following for permission to reproduce photographs:
Ardea: J Daniels pp**17**, **24**, A Warren p**19**; Bruce Coleman Ltd: I Arndt p**18**, G Cubitt p**8**, C and D Frith p**10**, A Purcell p**14**, Dr F Sauer p**4**; Corbis/DK Ltd: pp**18**, **20**; Garden and Wildlife Matters: pp**5**, **21**, **23**, **29**; NHPA: R Fotheringham p**22**; Okapia: O Cabrero I Roura p**15**, U Gross p**12**; Oxford Scientific Films: H Abipp p**11**, G Bernard pp**7**, **9**, **27**, **28**, D Clyne/Mantis Wildlife Films p**6**, J Cooke p**25**, Z Leszczynski/ Animals Animals p**13**, R Mendez/Animals Animals p**16**, P Parkes p**26**.

Cover photograph reproduced with permission of Photolibrary.com/Oxford Scientific Films/John Mitchell

The publishers would like to thank Nancy Harris for her assistance in the preparation of this book.

The paper used to print this book comes from sustainable resources.

Any words appearing in the text in bold, **like this**, are explained in the Glossary

Contents

What are centipedes?

Centipedes are small animals with lots of legs. They are invertebrates. This means they have no backbone.

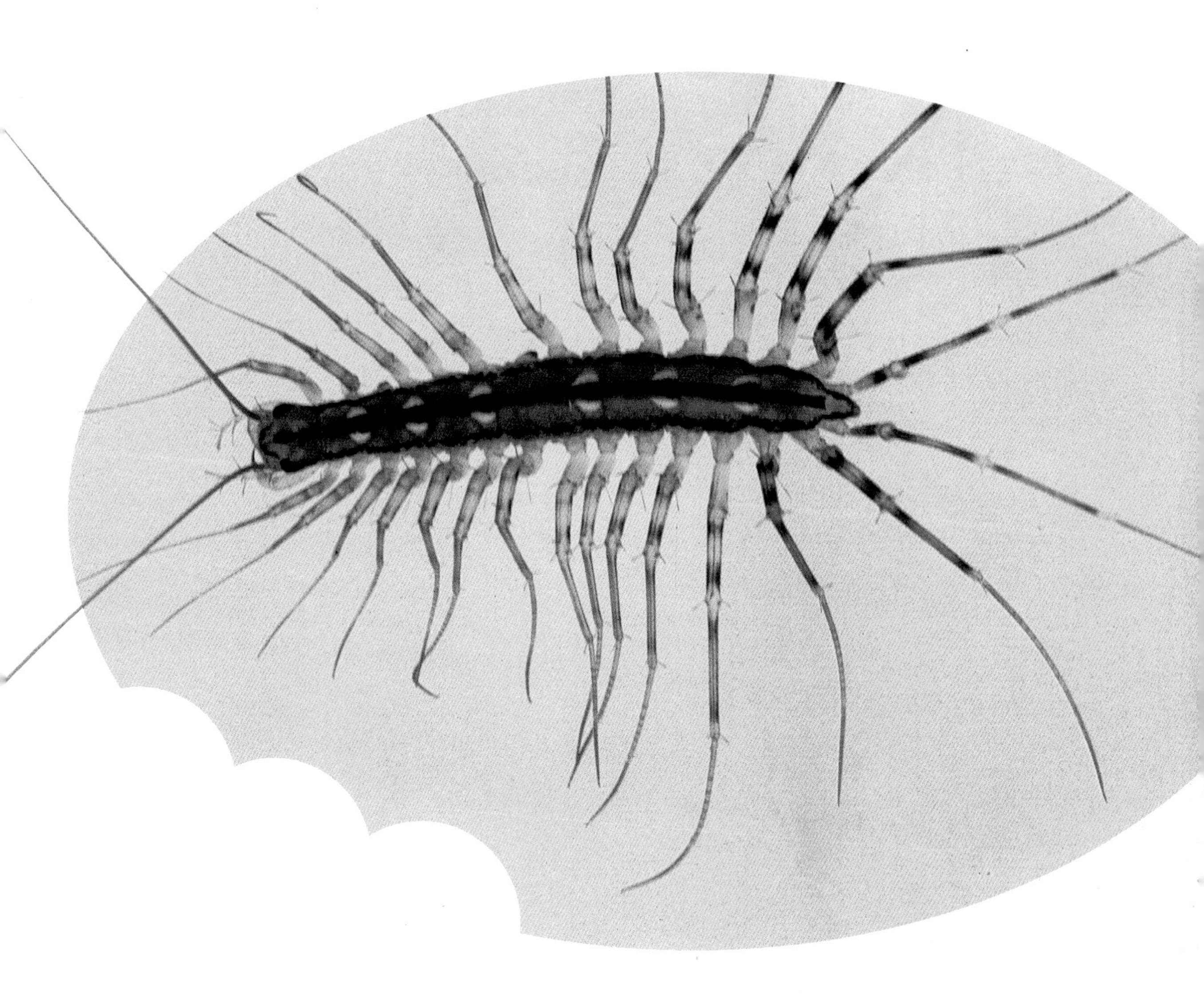

There are many different types of centipede. They live all over the world.

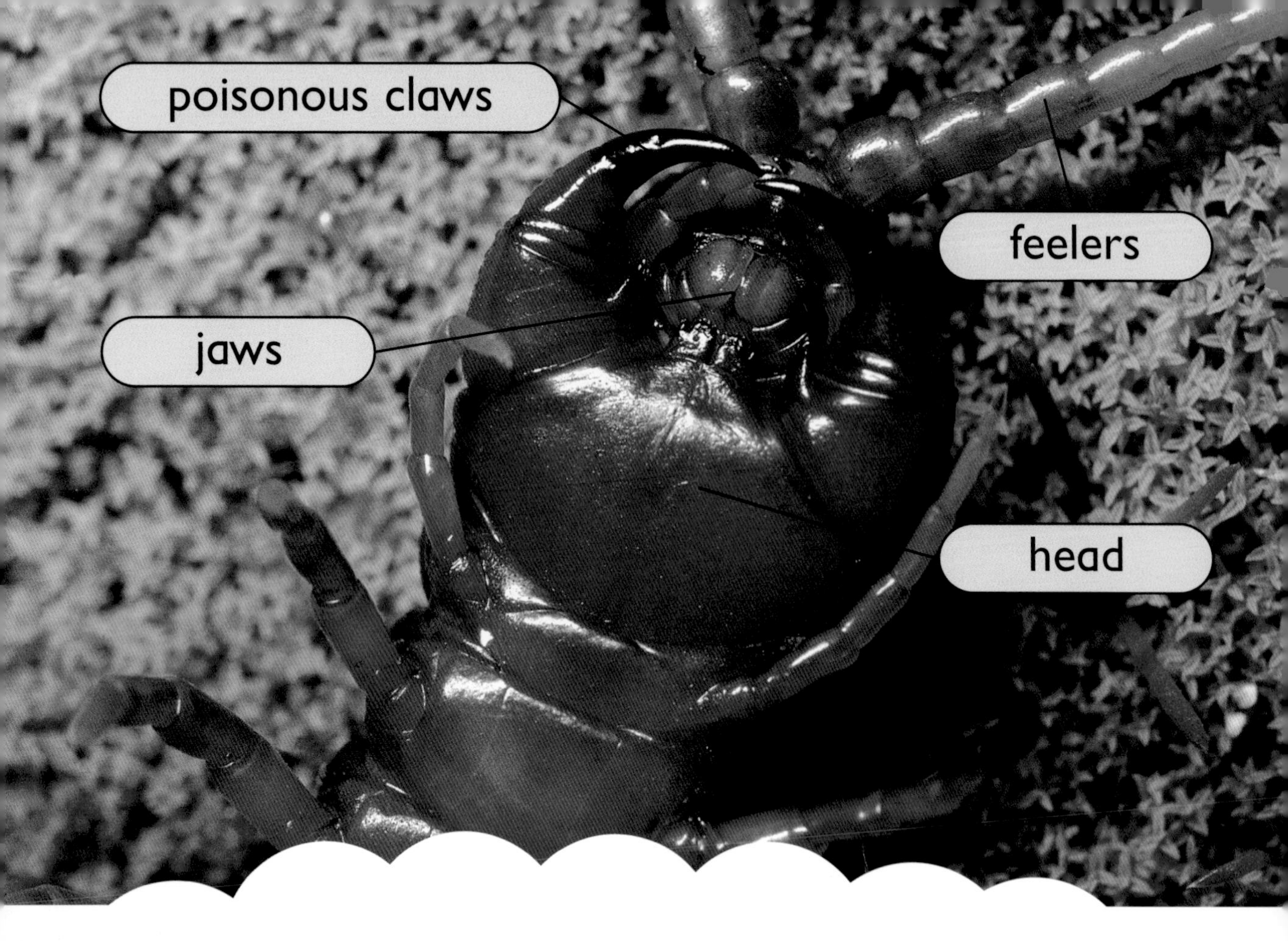

Centipedes have long bodies. They have a head with a pair of **feelers**. There are two poisonous claws at the back of the head. They have big jaws for biting.

Centipedes' bodies are made up of rings called **segments**. Each segment has two legs. Centipedes are often dark brown. If they live in the soil they are pale brown.

Centipedes can be different sizes. The smallest centipedes have 15 pairs of legs. Big ones can have as many as 177 pairs.

Centipedes that live in cool countries can grow as long as your little finger. Centipedes that live in hot countries can be nearly as long as your arm.

How are centipedes born?

In spring the **male** and **female** centipedes **mate**. The female lays eggs in a hole. She curls her body around her eggs to protect them.

A stone centipede rolls her eggs in the soil. Little lumps of soil stick to the eggs and hide them from **predators**.

When the eggs **hatch** the centipedes are very small. The babies grow quickly and soon their skin is too small for them.

They wriggle out of their old skins. There is a new skin underneath. This is called **moulting**. The new skin has more body **segments** with new legs.

What do centipedes eat?

Centipedes are **predators**. This means they hunt other small animals. They use their poisonous claws to kill worms, spiders and some insects.

This centipede is eating a moth. Centipedes sometimes eat fruit or potatoes too.

Which animals eat centipedes?

Some creatures, such as large beetles, hunt centipedes. Some birds like to eat centipedes too.

When we see blackbirds pecking the ground or digging with their beaks, they are looking for food. Sometimes they find a centipede to eat.

How do centipedes move?

Centipedes have **joints** between their body **segments** so they can bend. Centipedes that live underground can wriggle into tiny cracks.

Some centipedes can move very quickly. They use their longer back legs to push themselves forward.

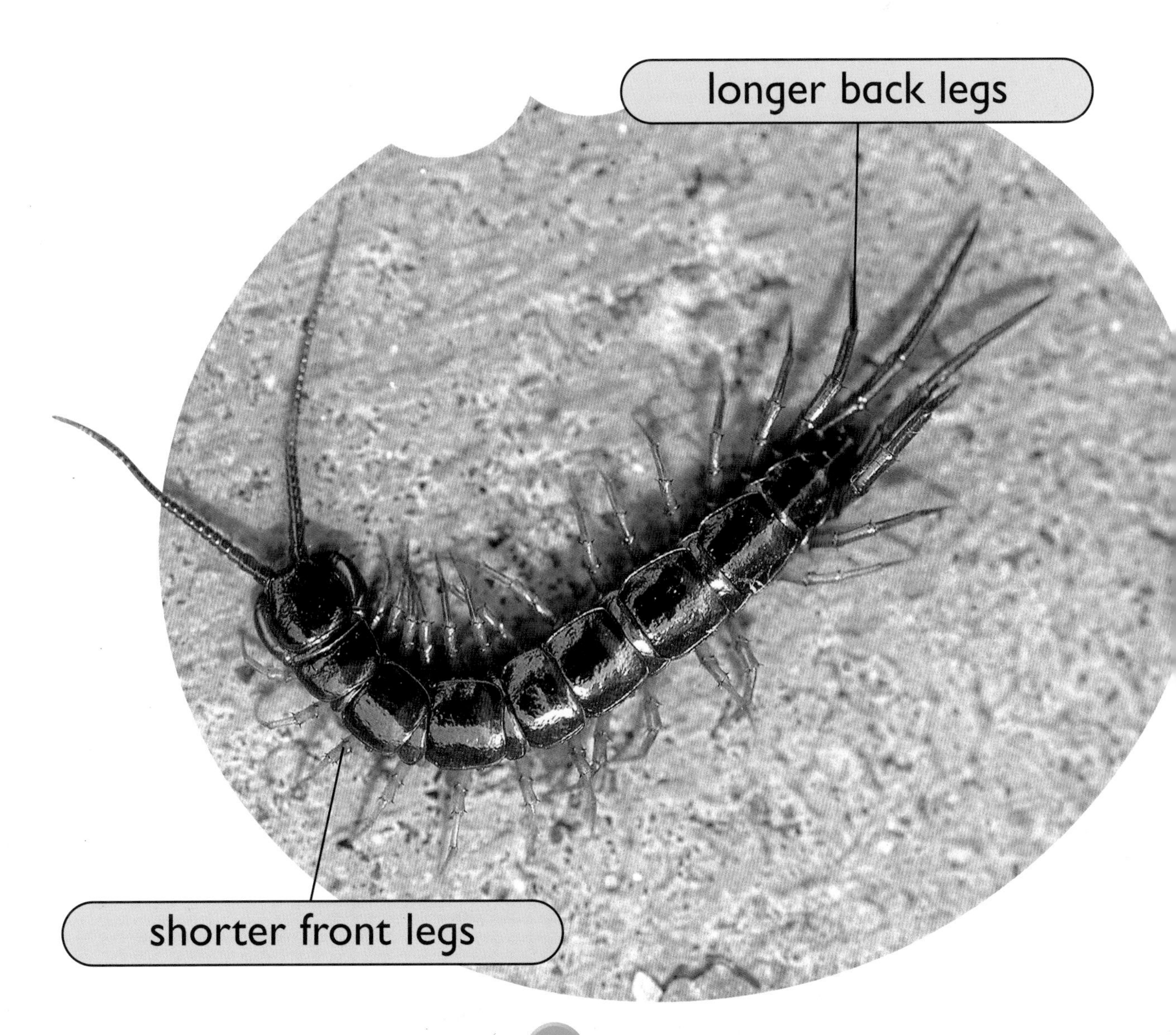

Where do centipedes live?

Centipedes like to live where it is damp and out of the sun. Some of the big centipedes live in hot rainforests.

In gardens, centipedes live under stones or under a shed. They can live in a heap of leaves or a rotting log. Others live in the soil.

How long do centipedes live?

If they are safe and warm, centipedes can live for more than five years.

Sometimes centipedes cannot find enough food to eat in the winter. They sleep underground until warmer weather comes. This is called **hibernating**.

What do centipedes do?

Most centipedes are helpful to gardeners. They kill many garden **pests**. Pests harm garden plants.

Some centipedes give a painful, poisonous bite if they are upset.

How are centipedes special?

Centipedes are **nocturnal**. This means they usually only come out at night. This is because the sun dries out their skin.

Some centipedes have no eyes. They find food by feeling the earth move when other small creatures are near. They smell and taste with their **feelers**.

Thinking about centipedes

Remember that some centipedes cannot see. How do you think they find their way around?

What do you think would happen to a centipede that stayed out in the sun on a warm summer's day? Where do centipedes like to live?

Bug map

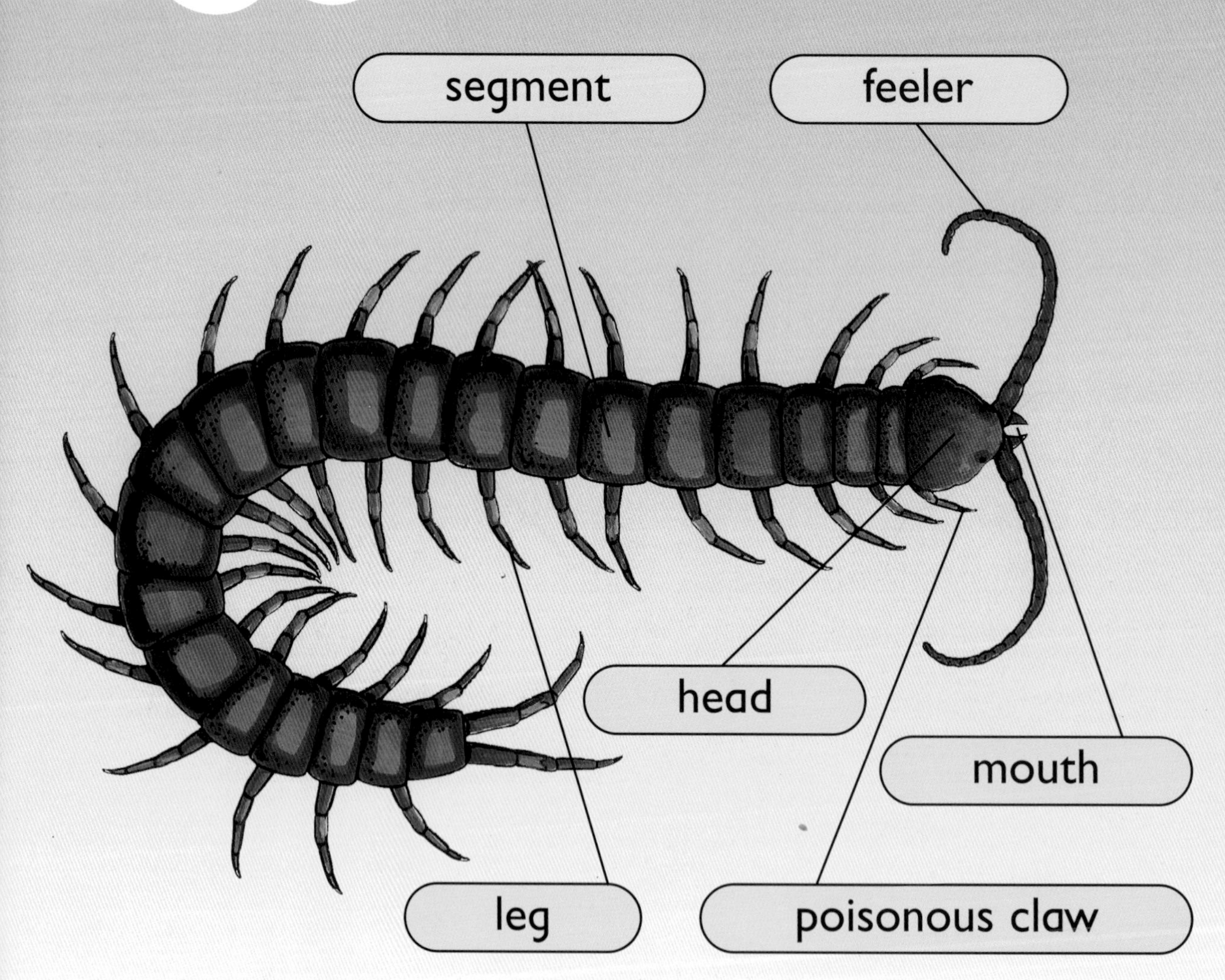

Glossary

feelers thin growths from the head of a centipede that help it to feel, smell and taste

female a girl

hatch to come out of an egg

hibernating sleeping through the winter months

joint a part of the body that lets it bend

male a boy

mate when male and female centipedes join up to make baby centipedes

moult when a centipede grows too big for its skin it grows a new one and wriggles out of its old skin

nocturnal an animal that sleeps in the day and comes out at night

pests animals that are a nuisance to people

predator animal that hunts other animals

segments small pieces of the body that are joined together one behind the other

Index

More books to read

Spiders, Centipedes and Millipedes,
Sally Morgan (Chrysalis Education, 2000)